An Angel's Touch

Inspired Writings
By
Sandra J Yearman

SERAPHIM PUBLISHING LLC

WE WILL BRING LIGHT TO ALL THE DARK PLACES

Registered trademark-
Sandra J Yearman
Seraphim Publishing
438 Water St. Cambridge, WI 53523

Copyright © 2011 Sandra J Yearman
Produced in the United States of America
Author : Sandra J Yearman
Editor: Sandra J Yearman
Cover Design by Sandra J Yearman
Layout and design by Sandra J Yearman

All rights reserved. No part of this book may be reproduced, stored in or introduced into a retrieval system, or transmitted, in any form or by any means, electronic or mechanical, including photocopying or recording or otherwise copied for public or private use—other than for "fair use" as brief quotations embodied in articles and reviews-without written permission from the author.

Library of Congress Control Number: 2011901920

ISBN: 978-0-9841506-7-0

First Edition

God Blesses Us With Angels
They Come In Any Guise
He Sends Us Love And Strength
And Blessings From The Skies
Amen
Amen
Amen

Contents

Dedication

To Touch An Angel..7
The Spirit And The Key..11
Kelly's Song..13
Here Am I 14
Christmas Tide...17
God Bless The Creatures.......................................19
Courage And Grace...21
In God I Have No Regrets....................................24
Christmas Night..26

Seeking Light In The Darkness

The Day That God Was Judged............................29
Rescue..32
In This World Of Conformity...............................34
God Bless The Warriors This Christmas..............36
Passing Of A Pet-An Extraordinary Friend..........38
A Mother's Tear..40
The World I Knew Betrayed Me...........................43
Images Of Hell..45

Contents

How Can The Light Of Faith Go Out...................47
There is Always Hope In The Darkness................49
That He Is Real..51
Memories That We Cherish 55
To Give Her Choices..57
Write My Mother...59
A Warrior's Journey...61
Tears Of Saints And Angels................................63
Find You In The Darkness..................................65

Coming Home

You Should Seek...70
It Is For The Love Of God..................................71
Spiritual Journeys..73
Mercy.. 75
On This Christmas Morning...............................82
My Friend Was Heaven Sent..............................84
The Flute And The Harp....................................87
An Angel's Touch...89

Dedication

To Touch An Angel

The little boy was crying
He was lost in this place
So many people passed him by
No one ever saw his face

Dirty and shivering
They were busy, they were late
The little boy stood crying
They never cared about his fate

He went into a building
Dark as it was cold
No one lived there
The building was so old

His head he buried
In his wet and torn sleeves
He cried for his parents
Why did they ever leave

Slowly he was awaken
By a voice and yet a dream
He saw a face before him
He was too afraid to scream

As the voice spoke to him
He was filled with love
It was the first time he felt safe
A blessing from above

When the Angel touched him
All his fears erased
She wiped away his tears
And blessed him with her Grace

'This is the Christmas season'
'When God sends miracles here'
'I have come to help you'
'To wipe away your tears'

He held to her
He hugged her with his might
She kissed him on the forehead
And took him from his fright

She carried him from that building
She took him to a home
Where he would always be loved
And never be alone

'This is the Christmas season'
'When God sends miracles here'
'I have come to help you'
'To wipe away your tears'

Amen Amen Amen

The Spirit And The Key

The Lion, The Lamb
The Great I AM

The Songs of Praise
From death were raised

The Spirit, the Key
The Holy Trinity

The mirror and the mask
Man's daunting tasks

Love from above
The Spirit, the Dove

All Heaven reigns
Life to begin again

Amen Amen Amen

Kelly's Song

Sing a song of kindness
Heard throughout the earth
The compassion you have shown
Fills the Angels hearts with mirth

Daily we have choices
To rise above this world
To be exceptional
With glee the Angels herald

Thank you for your kindness
And your loving attitude
My heart is overwhelmed
With feelings of gratitude

Amen Amen Amen

Here Am I

'Who will I send', cried the Voice
from Heaven
'Who will I send', said the Voice
on High
From the darkness below came a voice
'My Lord, here am I'

'Here am I', cried the voice to Heaven
'Here am I', cried the voice through
tears
'I will go before You'
'Your Song to sing through all my
years'

'You have been a faithful servant'
'You have walked the paths that
 I decree'
'You have cried out to the Heavens'
'A world to save upon your knees'

'I will Bless you with this mission'
'I will send you through the stars'
'I will walk with you always'
'For my son, blessed you are'

'Here am I', cried the voice to Heaven
'Here am I', cried the voice through tears
'I will go before You'
'Your Song to sing through all my years'

The Lord Blessed Isaiah
And gave him words to speak
To a world dying in its darkness
A brighter path to seek

'Here am I', cried the voice to Heaven
'Here am I', cried the voice through tears
'I will go before You'
'Your Song to sing through all my years'

Amen Amen Amen

Christmas Tide

A Light came through the darkness
A Song so sweet and pure
It healed the human frailties
In this most miraculous time of year

It touched the hearts of many
It sang to them the Song
It filled the lives with Love and Grace
It filled the dreams they longed

The darkness could not withstand
This Light, from Heaven sent
Which filled the world with Love and Hope
As only God had meant

Glory Alleluia
Praises sing on High
To God of all the worlds
Whose Light fills the skies

Glory Alleluia
Praises that we sing
May God of all the worlds
His Glory, here to bring

Amen Amen Amen

God Bless The Creatures

God Bless the creatures
That others may see
The Grace of God
In gifts from Thee

To love and to nurture
To care and to tend
To love without boundaries
Is the Grace that God sends

The hearts that are touched
With an Angel's hand
Protects the creatures
In this world of man

To love without judging
To give without motive
To be grateful for all
God's Grace to give

Amen Amen Amen

Courage And Grace

The baby Angel travelled
To a place where she had never been
A hospital filled with patients
Hearts where terror dwelled within

She was confused at first
Why would God send her there
Until she looked about her
And felt the fear within the air

Everyone was dying
Although in different degrees
In Spirit and in body
The Angel prayed upon her knees

Father, now I understand
Thank You for using me in this way
Let us heal these people
Let them find a better Way

I pray that Your Presence
Touches every soul and being
Let them feel Your Love
Let them know the meaning

That God will always carry
That God will always heal
That God will Bless us with His Love
To ask and to kneel

The baby Angel touched and cried
And Prayed for all in that place
She asked for God the Father
To bless them with His Grace

And in that hectic hospital
Filled with fear and sorrow
No one realized the miracles
That healed their tomorrows

Amen Amen Amen

In God I Have No Regrets

While walking on this journey
I dwelt upon my life
I was tired of being afraid
Conquered by my strife

I called out to the Heavens
To take away my fear
And in an answer to my prayer
The Presence of God was brought near

God, I would beseech Thee
To fill me with Your Grace
To save me from myself
And the darkness of this place

I talked to God all evening
The day and then the night
And as the sun rose in the sky
I was no longer a slave unto my fright

In that early morning
The starlight from the east
God carried me above my fears
And saved me from the beast

When my heart is hallowed
And pure are my requests
God answers all that I would pray
In God I have no regrets

Amen Amen Amen

Christmas Night

God on this night of mystery
Wonder at Your Birth
Send Your Grace upon us
Send Your Peace to earth

There are wars raging
There is chaos in this world
Let the Song of Christmas
By Angels be herald

Let Your children remember
The Love of Your Birth
The greatest gift God could send
To bless His children on earth

Let us choose to emulate
The Life and yet the Word
The Love and Grace of Heaven
In our hearts be stirred

Amen Amen Amen

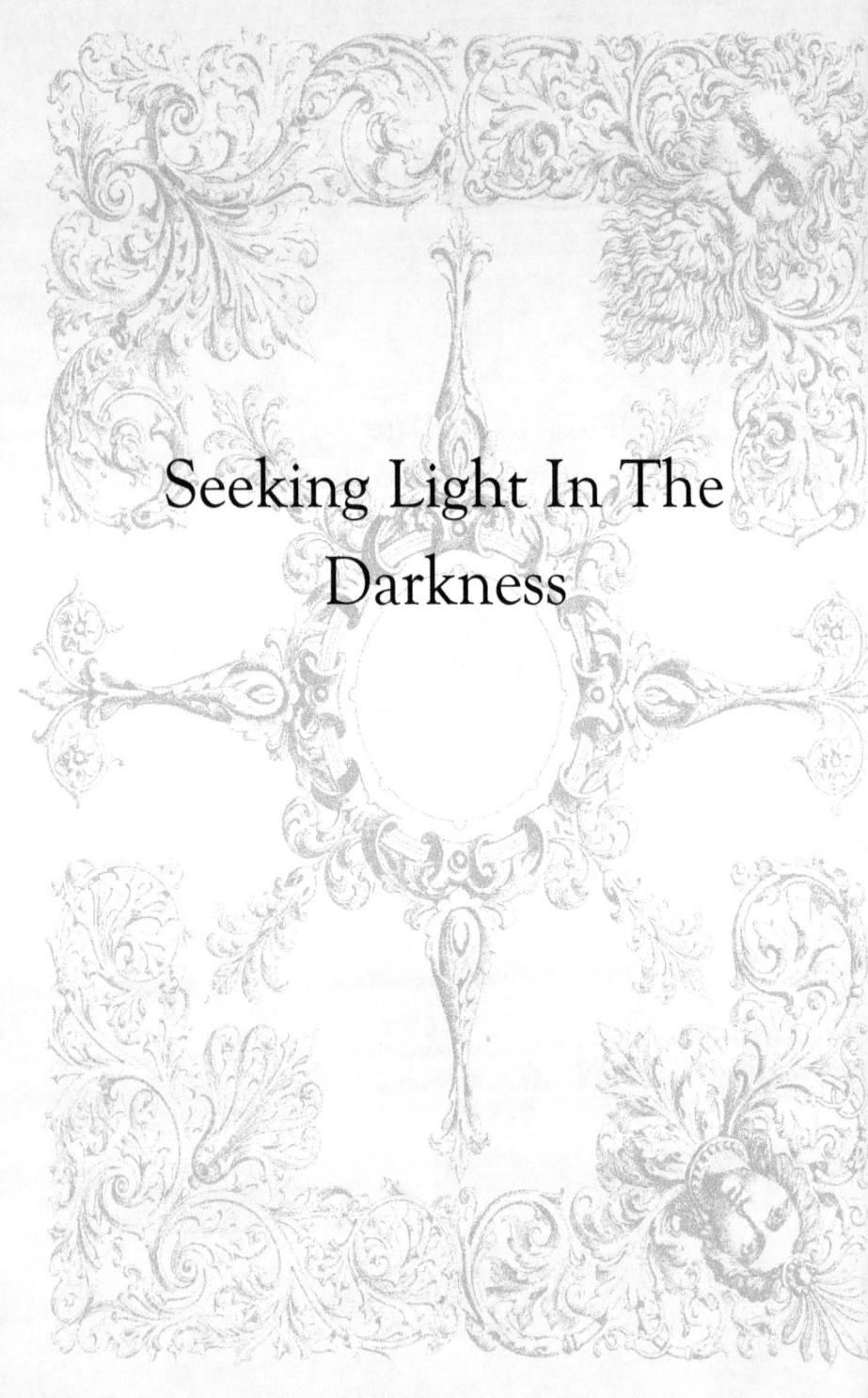

Seeking Light In The Darkness

The Day That God Was Judged

Today I heard a story
That shocked me with disgrace
The day that God was judged
By the human race

Filled they were with anger
Hatred and fear
They transferred their darkness
On the God we hold dear

Just as in the time of Jesus
They accused Him of the actions
of man
They transferred their darkness
Did not anyone take a stand

Was it in a court room
Or court yard of a king
Was it in a circus
Or the hearts of human beings

How many mirrors must God hold up
Before we see our true faces
Yet we accuse Eternal Holiness
Of our own disgraces

Is it our guilt we cannot live with
Or our fear of the demons that we call
Do we feel empowered
By accusing the Great All

God forgive Your children
That they may see
The Grace and Blessings
of Your Presence
The Love that is sent from Thee

Amen Amen Amen

Rescue

He could not walk
She could not stand
Abuse they suffered
At man's hands

Flesh that was torn
Wounds not healed
The ego of man
Would force them to kneel

What has brought us
To such a place
Void of Mercy
Void of Grace

God save the victims
Of darkness and greed
Stand before them
With Your Holy Creed

Amen Amen Amen

In This World Of Conformity

In this world of conformity
God there is a prayer that
I would ask
Please give me the courage
To walk in my own path

Destinies determined
Scripts are Heaven sent
Please give me the integrity
To choose a life as it was meant

Although I hear the voices
Their songs are not always right
Please give me the strength
To rise above the chaos of the night

Help me to make choices
That bring me into the Light
Help me to know my purpose
Keep me in Your Sight

So that the journey I am taking
Will take me to the stars
Will free me from my chains
Will lead me, oh so far

Amen Amen Amen

God Bless The Warriors This Christmas

God Bless the warriors
Who stand before
This great country
From shore to shore

Bless them this Christmas
That they may know
The love that is sent
Which many do not show

God let them know
That many think of
Their courage and loyalty
Their patriotism and love

Protect them in the course
of their duties
Walk with them in the night
Comfort and heal
Their terror and fright

God at this Christmas time
Fill them with Grace
Let them know they are loved
And missed from the places

Of a life they left
To guard and to protect
We salute them all
With honor and respect

Amen Amen Amen

Passing Of A Pet
An Extraordinary Friend

We have been together
Lives so entwined
A better friend God would send
In this world I would not find

Are pets mirrors of our souls
Or that missing piece
Are they Angels sent from Heaven
To give us Love and Release

From the darkness we are drawn to
From the pain this life can bring
Pets embody love
Their souls to us do sing

God fill the void created
When my friend left me all alone
When his time had ended
When he returned back Home

Help me keep the lessons
That he taught and that he lived
Love has no boundaries
To receive you have to give

Amen Amen Amen

A Mother's Tear

She sacrificed her mind and body
And the life that she had here
To care for her family
The ones who she held dear

The lines of age on her face
Showed the world, that she
Laughed and cried with life
Praying often to Thee

Years that passed, the family grew
With love the duties done
The children never questioned
The mother's life as one

Left they did, without regret
Lives they must pursue
Yet did they ever thank her
Or give her the credit she was due

Time throughout the ages
We cannot control
When one is abandoned
The loneliness takes its toll

Tied to a chair, so she will not fall
Crying for her 'mama' dear
She calls out to the others
Who pretend they do not hear

God thank you for our families
The lives with which we are blessed
Keep our hearts filled with love
That we may pass the tests

That we may remember and cherish
That we may treat with Grace
That we may take the hand
That needs to be held in this place

Amen Amen Amen

The World I Knew Betrayed Me

The blood that I was soaked in
Was a comrade's I adored
The horror that beget me
I cried out to the Lord

'Please save my friend and brother'
'Please save this warrior's life'
'Let him return to his home'
'To his children and his wife'

In my arms I cradled
The life that was my friend
I cried and prayed together
That this was not the end

My tears would not stop flowing
For the sadness that I felt
The world I knew betrayed me
The deadly blow was dealt

As I prayed to Heaven
I felt his life return
The answers were before me
The miracles that I yearned

I put it all in His Hands
For there was nothing else I could do
My earthly strength was lost
The miracles I prayed for; rang True

Amen Amen Amen

Images Of Hell

The fear I saw in their eyes
Will stay with me all my days
The anguish in their voices
Their eyes clouded by haze

The fear that consumed them
Disfigured and fed
The darkness, the cancers
The lives they had led

Ageless forever
The tolls darkness takes
Bodies gnarled
By demons and hate

I saw a woman
Who walked with the dead
Her life long gone
A shadow instead

God save Your children
From the choices they make
From their darkest desires
Their greed and their hate

God wake their hearts
To Your Grace and Your Love
That they may remember their Father
And their Home above

Amen Amen Amen

How Can The Light Of Faith Go Out

'How can the Light of Faith go out'
The baby Angel asked
Confused by the world she saw
The darkness and the masks

God did not answer
He waited for her to reply
A smile came across her face
'This world is dark, but here am I'

'So this is why You sent me'
'So this is why I am here'
'To dispel this darkness'
'To help them overcome the fear'

'Then I will raise my voice for many'
'Who are afraid to speak'
'God please enter this world'
'Your Holiness we seek'

'My wings can shelter many'
'And through Your Grace even more'
'Let Your Light shine through me'
'To help this world to soar'

Amen Amen Amen

There Is Always Hope In The Darkness

Let us sing a song of healing
Let us sing a song of Grace
To the diseased and to the dying
To the burdened and to the disgraced

There is always Hope in the darkness
There is always Love in the night
Put your Faith in God
Our problems to make right

When your burden is too heavy
The weight more than you can bear
Put your Faith in God
Your problems to share

When the way is so dreary
And you are weakened by life
Call out to the Heavens
To carry your strife

There is always Hope in the darkness
There is always Love in the night
Put your Faith in God
Our problems to make right

Amen Amen Amen

That He Is Real

I thought my body betrayed me
I was filled with confusion and fear
I wanted to separate from it
I wanted my life which I held dear

This disease would overtake me
Obliterate the life that I enjoyed
All that I have built would vanish
All that I am would be destroyed

The anger welled within me
I could not understand
Why I was the target
Of this curse of man

Then one day an Angel
Tiny as a child
Spoke to me through my darkness
And said 'walk with me for a while'

With her gentle spirit
And the Love that she sent forth
I realized I had wandered
Completely off my course

I had let the darkness consume me
And define who I would be
I thought my strength was
in what I built
Instead of putting my faith in Thee

Father I call to Heaven
Please restore Your Light in me
That I may break through the darkness
of this world
That I may truly see

Eradicate the darkness within me
That it may not pollute
The holy vessel You created
With an unholy substitute

Father have Mercy on me
Heal my frail being
Cleanse me with the Grace of Heaven
Help me to understand the
true meaning

That God will strengthen
That God will heal
That He will guard
That He is real

Amen Amen Amen

Memories That We Cherish

I reflected on the year that passed
And sadness stirred my being
For so much death had occurred
I allowed it to affect my way of seeing

Years do come and years do go
And some stay with you forever
The memories of all I lost
Their faces I will always remember

Memories that we cherish
Can take us to the past
Where we can get lost forever
An illusion that will not last

At times it is hard to remember
That our lives we have to live
True love is eternal
When our hearts we do give

God help me to remember
That perception is a gift
Help me not to sink into darkness
But help my spirit to lift

Instead of allowing my pain
To fill me with despair
I should sing praise to Heaven
For their lives I was allowed to share

Amen Amen Amen

To Give Her Choices

She sat in the darkness
Afraid to look in the mirror
The demons she saw there
Filled her with fear

Afraid of the future
Afraid of the past
She sat in the darkness
Wearing a demon's mask

Filled with hatred
No one came near
Her anger and viciousness
Filled others with fear

The Light of an Angel
Drew her attention
But she attacked and attacked
And fought an ascension

God sent the Angel
To give her choices
But she fought the Angel
And listened to the demon's voices

The Angel waited
For many years
But she chose to sit in the darkness
Filled with her fears

Amen Amen Amen

Write My Mother

Write my mother
The soldier gasped
As he held the medic
With his weakened grasp

Tell her I love her
And that I am sorry for
The anger and yelling
And so much more

If I could do it all again
My heart would override my pride
I would say the things that need
to be said
Before the moment I am to die

And in this world
Of horror and fear
I would talk to God
And bring the Angels near

For now I see them
And at last
My life is clear
I can heal my past

Amen Amen Amen

A Warrior's Journey

The mysteries of existence
The trials and tests are known
Only to our Holy King
Upon the Holy Throne

We wonder on this journey
About the trials we meet
Often never thinking
They form a path to that we seek

We wonder about our lives here
Are they planned or are they fate
Do we have a reason
A purpose we must sate

Is there more to life here
Other worlds to know
Are we judged on actions
Have we seeds to sow

God guide me on this journey
Bless me with the tests
That I might seek and grow
And realize how I am blessed

For in the hills and valleys
The tempests and the storms
I have discovered more
This existence to transform

Amen Amen Amen

Tears Of Saints And Angels

Tears of saints and Angels
Tears of Heaven flow
The compassion of God
For His children here, below

How often do we hear Him
His Voice, our hearts to speak
Does fear drown Him out
Or Holiness to seek

Would the tears of Heaven
Cleanse the darkness here
Will the children of God
Stop calling demons near

Will the Voice ever waiver
Will the tears cease to flow
Will the children of God
His Holiness to know

Amen Amen Amen

Find You In The Darkness

She stumbled in the darkness
The cold wind bit her cheeks
She was searching for some kindness
This tortured soul to meet

A light she spied in the dark night
It seemed so far away
She had been travelling so long
She did not think she could make
another day

The wind started howling
The snow blinded her eyes
She tripped and fell onto the ground
Her voice quivered as she cried

The cold it overtook her
She started to drift away
When a voice whispered to her
'You will see another day'

The warmth started to fill her
The pain, it went away
She felt a loving touch
She wanted it to stay

'I think that she is waking'
'You gave us such a fright'
'What is a girl like you'
'Doing out on such a night'

The words did not come to her
She did not understand
How she came into this home
With this woman and this man

When her voice had gathered
It was strained and it was weak
'How did I get here'
'Were the only words she could speak'

'My dear don't you remember'
'Your friend who brought you here'
'He laid you by the fire'
'And whispered into your ear'

'He was gone in just a moment'
'He didn't say his name'
'He didn't say where he was going'
'Or from whence he came'

'But he did leave you something'
'A strange gift that it is'
'A single white feather'
'He said that it was his'

'He said for you to keep it'
'And whenever you were frightened in the night'
'He would find you in the darkness'
'And protect you with God's might'

Amen Amen Amen

Coming Home

You Should Seek

You should seek is the answer
To questions unknown
The Course is before you
The destinies sown

Stars from the Heavens
As breadcrumbs on a path
The Way is before you
That will forever last

Gifts sent from Heaven
Answers received
Blessed are the children
Blessed are those who Believe

Amen Amen Amen

It Is For The Love Of God

It is for the love of God that I take this journey
It is for the love of God that I sing
It is for the love of God that I teach these words
His Holiness to bring

May the Holy Spirit consume His children
May His Grace ignite their paths
May the Angels hover over
May God Bless our every task

Let man remember
The time before their hearts were sold
To darkness for greed and power
The nightmares, the prophets foretold

So let us live with Honor
And transcend the curse of man
It is for the love of God that I take
this journey
Grasp His outreached Hand

Amen Amen Amen

Spiritual Journeys

I had to brave the darkness
I had to conquer the fears
I had to walk through the fire
To face that holy mirror

The tests that I have taken
The journeys I have been
I would not change one moment
I would do them all again

Was it in the seeking
Or the lessons that I learned
The choices that I made
The holy path I yearned

That the darkness that surrounded
Chipped and fell away
Exposing the light within me
To show me a better Way

Amen Amen Amen

Mercy

The Pharisee had travelled
Weary from his ride
He sought shelter in a village
A home he went inside

He demanded that they serve him
He told them of his name
The power that he held
The family from which he came

He bragged about his riches
And his monopoly on grace
He said that God recognized
The superiority of his race

He told the family of the home
That God only listened to men
of power
And that if they would serve him
He would intervene on their last hour

The family in their graciousness
Served him the last of their food
Such a generous gesture
The Pharisee never understood

During his dinner
A daughter yet a child
Stood by the table
Watched him all the while

Small she was for her age
Frail was her frame
The Pharisee annoyed
Finally asked for her name

She said my name is Mercy
And asked if he was a holy man
She said that she was dying
And there were some things she
wanted to understand

The two of them talked for hours
Long into the night
She asked him many questions
But he only revealed his terror
and fright

He mocked her for her faith in God
Because he felt she should fear death
He said she should feel cheated
And blame God with her last breath

She listened to him quietly
Looking at the darkness in his eyes
She felt the coldness of his heart
She knew he spoke in lies

Finally she answered
With the voice only an Angel knew
Sir while you were speaking
I said a prayer for you

You see I feel a Presence
It is with me everyday
I know it is God
And I ask Him to stay

The reason I do not fear death
Is because I feel great peace
I put my life in God's Hands
And feel genuine release

And I never feel cheated
I have a good life
I have always been loved
And God has carried me through
my strife

I have many blessings
Though they may pale compared
to yours
But I choose to have a grateful heart
And not to view life as having
to be endured

Please do not mock me
For not living a life of fear
I call out to the Heavens
And ask for God's Presence here

Never had the Pharisee
Met someone of true faith
Never had he heard a voice
Sing with Holy Grace

The little girl prayed for him
And blessed him with her might
The Pharisee left their home
To wander in the night

Amen Amen Amen

On This Christmas Morning

On this Christmas morning
A world is cleansed with Grace
For God has sent His Spirit
To bring His Blessings to this place

The Son He sent before us
To bring His miracles here
With the cry of that tiny voice
The Heavens were brought near

Years turn into centuries
In this world of man
Yet the Truth of God
All time, all worlds cannot withstand

Bless us with Your Mercy
Bless us with Your Grace
Bless us with the Peace of God
Our darkness to erase

Glory Alleluia
On this Christmas morn
Glory Alleluia
The Son of God is born

Amen Amen Amen

My Friend Was Heaven Sent

Lying in the darkness
The illusion weighing on my soul
I felt a presence with me
A Holiness foretold

A form and yet a whisper
Her red hair floated in the night
The love I felt from her
Eased the burden of my fright

Familiar was her presence
She called me by name
I recognized her voice
The one and the same

That had whispered on the night air
That had sang to me a song
That watched me in the darkness
That had been with me lifelong

A friend and yet a guardian
A guide in the darkness of the night
That showed herself to me
At the height of my fright

I calmed when I saw her
I knew she was Heaven sent
Her presence at this time
Took the fear from this event

Long has my life been here
The journey as it was meant
And whenever I needed help
My friend was Heaven sent

Amen Amen Amen

The Flute And The Harp

The flute, the harp
The music played
To honor God
In far gone days

A king who wrote
For the King who Created
Songs of praise
To God were celebrated

The flute, the harp
The music sang
And uplifted hearts
In the world of man

Listen closely
And you will hear
King David play
To bring the Heavens near

Amen Amen Amen

An Angel's Touch

He sat in the darkness
Fear gripped his soul
No one understood his journey
No one knew the tolls

Always in control
No one ever knew he was weak
Afraid to let them know
Afraid to be meek

His fear built a wall
With no gate and no key
To keep others out
Now he would never be free

An Angel kept watching
And imploring to God
'Let me go into the darkness'
'Where this man has trod'

God sent the Angel
Into the darkness of man
To comfort this soul
To take his hand

Disguised as a child
The man did not know
That the friend he had made
Would save his very soul

God sends us Angels
To touch and to reprieve
To heal us and guide us
The Spirit to receive

Amen Amen Amen

There Is Always Hope
In The Darkness
There Is Always Love In The Night
Put Your Faith In God
Our Problems To Make Right
Amen
Amen
Amen

www.ingramcontent.com/pod-product-compliance
Lightning Source LLC
Chambersburg PA
CBHW051708040426
42446CB00008B/780